T0146878

HOOSIER HYSTERIA
A '67 Griffith Panther Memoir

HOOSIER HYSTERIA
A '67 Griffith Panther Memoir

RICK BUTLER

HOOSIER HYSTERIA - A '67 GRIFFITH PANTHER MEMOIR

iUniverse books may be ordered through booksellers or by contacting:

iUniverse
1663 Liberty Drive
Bloomington, IN 47403
www.iuniverse.com
1-800-Authors (1-800-288-4677)

ISBN: 978-1-5320-0356-1 (sc)
ISBN: 978-1-5320-0299-1 (e)

Library of Congress Control Number: 2016912047

Print information available on the last page.

iUniverse rev. date: 09/12/2016

This book is dedicated to my wife, Judy Butler, my best friend, Marty, the memories of Pete, my beloved grandpa, Earl, and my mother, Martha.

Judy (Urevig) Butler and I started going together in our senior year of high school, and she became the love of my life. We were engaged during my leave from the army just prior to going to Vietnam and were married eleven days after I returned. I was a mess after returning from Vietnam, but Judy was there for me at Fort Knox as I tried to put Vietnam behind me. To make matters worse, I came down with two types of malaria at Fort Knox four months after we were married. We made many sacrifices and lived like paupers to enable me to get through college after the army. Although I ultimately was diagnosed with PTSD (post-traumatic stress disorder) and have been in therapy on and off over the years, I had a successful career in business. Judy has been there with me through all of this for over forty years. I still remember my buddies in Vietnam, all of whom said, "Forget about your girl back home. They never wait." Well, I guess they never knew Judy.

Marty is a lifelong best friend who I've known since little league baseball when I was ten. We spent hundreds of hours in pick-up basketball games played on the streets at our outdoor city courts in Griffith. We played high school basketball together for four years. And to this day we maintain our long-distance relationship through periodic phone calls and visits that have spanned hundreds of miles over the years.

Pete (November 27, 1948, to July 11, 2008) was a great friend, classmate, and basketball player. I met Pete in kindergarten and played basketball with him on school teams starting in fifth grade through our senior year. I walked to and from school with him every day for four years of high school. He is dearly missed by all of his basketball buddies and classmates. Pete, thanks for the memories ...

Earl was my favorite grandpa and best friend until he died when I was ten years old. I spent a ton of time with Earl—listening to his never-ending stories, fishing, and playing games. I'd be willing to bet I spent more time with Earl in those first ten years of my life than the average kid would spend in their lifetime with their grandpa. Earl was a wonderful grandpa, and I still miss him dearly.

Martha Butler is my mom, who made the scrapbook for me, which was the basis for this book. Thanks, Mom, for everything

Contents

Preface

My name is Rick Butler, and I was a starting forward on the 1967 Griffith Panther's Indiana high school basketball team. We made school basketball history that year with a record of twenty wins and four losses. This is the story of my journey through Hoosier hysteria and the love for the game that landed me on that championship team.

Acknowledgments

The Hammond Times Newspaper—images of news stories and pictures of our team are featured throughout this book and were taken from a scrapbook created by my mother, Martha Butler, fifty years ago.

Kristin and Mark Gallagher—thanks for your support and editorial advice on my manuscript. Your ongoing encouragement kept me from giving up on this book.

My family Judy, Leslie, Doug, and Maya—thanks for listening to all the stories and for tediously plowing through multiple, changing manuscripts.

Cathy Fercik—thanks for the final bit of encouragement that caused me to publish this book

And last but certainly not least *Marty, Lenny, Pete, and Kerry*—thanks for being the talented basketball players that you were that led us all on this glorious ride through Hoosier hysteria

In Indiana basketball is not just a sport—it is a passion. Those who play it or watch it do so with reverence—*for the love of the game*!

—Author unknown

Chapter 1

The Early Years

Indiana basketball was special because after WWII it was the state's main sport. A lot of Indiana schools could not afford to field a football team. Indiana was primarily an agricultural state, and the basketball teams became the faces of the towns. Friday- and Saturday-night basketball was the winter social event between harvest and planting. The state was blessed with a large number of great coaches who knew they had to win to keep their jobs. It was also cheap entertainment for families who didn't have television yet. In fact radio made a big impact on making the forties, fifties, and sixties the golden age of Indiana basketball. All the small towns had a fifty-watt AM station that was controlling 100 percent of the listeners in its area. And these stations loved to air the high school basketball games. The coaching in Indiana was such that many colleges in the south and west would fill out their rosters with Indiana kids because they were grounded in the basics, could play defense, could shoot free-throws, and were extremely coachable. These Indiana kids knew the game.

The crown jewel of high school basketball in America was the Indiana state tournament. All the states around the Midwest had class tourneys (schools were slotted in tournament classes based on school size, with big schools playing each other and small schools playing small schools, etc.). There could be as many as seven state champs (one for each class), like in Illinois. In Indiana you had one class. Only one team could go undefeated. The state championship was a sellout for fifty-six straight years. When going to the sectional, it was a twelve- or sixteen-team tourney. It took four days, and everyone got time off from school to see afternoon games. If your school won a sectional, the school gave all the kids the following Monday off. Indiana went to class basketball in the early '80s, and it hasn't been the same since. To say Indiana high school basketball was a big deal in the '60s is a gross understatement.

In Indiana, love and passion for the game of basketball are known as Hoosier hysteria. This affliction affects the young and old alike. No one is immune, and they have never even tried to invent a vaccine.

It's hard to say when exactly I got my first dose of Hoosier hysteria. It could very well have started with my first shot at the rim that Dad nailed to a tree in the backyard on Wright Street. Or it could have been at the first basketball clinic I attended in fourth grade. But I had the affliction by the time I tried out and made my fifth-grade team. And I had it in spades as I played high school basketball all four years.

The kids who get afflicted with this hysteria have this overwhelming desire to play basketball almost all the time nearly year round. In grade school, at least 80 percent of the boys played basketball most of the time. There were basketball hoops all over our little town. Not only were they at playgrounds but also at most parking lots and on a lot of garages as well. Playing basketball comes in many sizes and shapes. It includes activities from just shooting around (shooting baskets) by yourself—to full-scale high school or college basketball at tournament time—and all variations in between. The most afflicted kids would even shovel snow off outside courts in the winter. The ball wouldn't bounce but you could shoot. Also in the winter it wasn't uncommon for many of us to have small rims and basketballs in our rooms for shooting or in the basement for one-on-one games

As for adults, they are not immune to this affliction, although it tends to affect them in different ways. Some may carry over their Hoosier hysteria from childhood. In those infrequent cases you will see these adults actually still playing the game. This can be in the form of over-thirty basketball leagues, pick-up games at the courts, or just shooting around at the courts or at basketball goals in their driveways.

Some go on to coach their kids in community basketball. But most of the adults with Hoosier hysteria just go bonkers following their local high school teams. And if their kids are on their high school team, the affliction goes beyond hysteria— approaching insanity. The symptoms of this type of affliction include attending as many games as possible, rooting wildly for their beloved players, and talking constantly about their team. This basketball talk occurs in many public places—on sidewalks, in stores, in bars, and of course, in barber shops. The barbers and patrons of these shops were incessant in their discussion and analysis of their teams and the games. And the talk would rise to a fevered frenzy if one of the basketball players came in for a haircut. I remember going in for haircuts my senior year. The questions were fast and furious: "Rick, how's the team doing? How are you doing? Are you going to win the next game? How's it looking for the sectional this year?" and so on. We were like celebrities—almost like gods. And of course we ate it up.

Basketball was so popular that everyone knew the game. Boys and girls alike—it didn't matter. And when the high school team had an away game, there were caravans of cars that went to those games, nearly emptying out the towns. Basketball was revered in these little Indiana towns. Our main courts in Griffith were on Broad Street—right smack in the middle of our town. There were six backboards, rims, and nets. And at times there were two full-court games going on simultaneously and still two other baskets for shooting or half-court games. And of course there were lights so we could play until nine or ten o'clock.

The basketball courts in the schools were even more highly regarded. They got a fresh coat of varnish in early October—just prior to the official start of tryouts and practice each year. And absolutely no street shoes were allowed on the floor. That's why the school dances were called "sock-hops." Everyone had to take off their shoes to dance in their socks.

It seemed inevitable that I would come down with Hoosier hysteria because Dad had a chronic dose of it. Dad had played high school varsity basketball for our same high school, Griffith. Who do you suppose nailed the rim on the backyard tree? Dad. There was no backboard, net, blacktop, or cement—just a hoop. But whoever said that Hoosier hysteria had to be fancy? And the rim was not just so I could shoot. My brother, Ken, shot baskets, as did Dad. Ken would shoot every once in a while, whereas Dad shot more often—a lot more often. Shooting baskets with them gave me something to do when I wasn't playing with the other kids in the neighborhood.

So by the time I was in the fourth grade, I had not only taken a liking to basketball, but I was also a good shot. It's not surprising that I was a good shot because most of my basketball playing was shooting in our backyard—sometimes shooting with Dad or Ken but more often by myself. When I had nothing to do, I'd go in the backyard and shoot around.

In fourth grade, when I found out there was going to be a basketball clinic at school on an upcoming Saturday I signed up. The clinic was not unlike the basketball camps of today. The emphasis was on fundamentals of both offense and defense. On offense they showed us how to shoot set shots, jump shots, and lay-ins and to dribble with both hands. They also had free-throw practice. On defense they emphasized the proper defensive position, foot work, keeping between the man you were guarding and the basket, and keeping your hands up. The clinic lasted about four hours, with the last hour being a scrimmage, or practice game.

There were no fourth-grade basketball teams. To play basketball, I had to go to the courts located in the center of town. By fourth grade, my family had moved, and there was not a basketball hoop at my house. But the public courts were only a block away. So I started going to the courts mostly to shoot baskets, but occasionally I was asked to play in pick-up games with the older kids.

One of the older kids, Rich, lived at the end of my block and had a basketball court inside his heated garage. Rich was on the junior high team, as were his buddies, all of whom played at Rich's garage. Occasionally, they would be short of players and would come and ask me to play. So I got to play in these games with kids two years older. When they picked up sides and picked me, they said I only counted as one half of a player because I was so young and small. Well one day I finally scored a basket, and a big debate ensued as to whether a basket from one half a player should count as one, two, or three points. They finally agreed it should count as two points, the same as the others. Everyone laughed, kind of at me, but I didn't care because I was getting valuable playing time with players far better than myself. Playing with players better than you makes you get better. And I did …

Chapter 2

Grade School

I n fifth grade the schools had basketball teams, so I decided to try out. I was just a weak, skinny little kid, so I was anxious and nervous about the tryouts. But my fears were unfounded. I not only made the team but was on the starting five. I was taller than many of the kids, so I played forward. I wasn't a big scorer, but I got my share of points and rebounds. I was fast and was good on defense. I also made the starting five on my sixth- and seventh-grade teams, and as a starter on the seventh-grade team, I got to dress for the eighth-grade games.

I guess I had the natural athletic ability to be a good basketball player, but surely one of the reasons for my success was practice. I played basketball pretty much all the time. The only other sport I was involved in was baseball. I played Little League and two years of Babe Ruth ball—until I was fourteen. Sure, we played pick-up baseball games during the summer, but I always found myself drawn to the basketball courts. The love for the game was in my blood.

Besides playing at the courts, a couple of other guys on the team had courts in their backyards, where pick-up games were regularly played. Occasionally I was invited to these courts but not often, as I was not good friends with them. This was unfortunate as most of the team players were involved in these games whereas I mostly shot baskets at the courts. So while the other guys were getting a lot of practice in pick-up games, I was mostly practicing my shooting. This made me a good shot when there was no defense against me, but it's quite another thing to make moves to create a shot with a defensive player on you. I also missed out on the invaluable benefit of pick-up games where you play offense and defense as a team. All of this unknowingly left me ill-prepared for the upcoming tryout.

When eighth-grade tryouts started, I felt somewhat confident because I had been a starter in seventh grade. But it didn't take long for me to realize that many of the other kids had passed me by, not in the areas of shooting and dribbling but for sure in the team aspects of the game, and this was especially evident during the tryout scrimmages. Tryouts lasted a week, and at the end of each day, the coach would post the names of the players still on the team. There were two cuts before the final one, and I had survived those first two. But each time I was relieved to see my name on the list. I made it to the final cut. On the day after the last day of tryouts, the final names were posted. I was afraid to look because I knew it was going to be extremely close.

Finally, at the end of the school day I went to the bulletin board and read the names. Mine was not there. I checked the names again and again and again but to no avail. I had been the last player cut. Though I had feared this, I still could not believe it. Tears welled up in my eyes, and I took off running out of the school and all the way home.

I went into my room, laid down on the bed, and cried. I felt as if my heart was broken. How could this have happened? Basketball was my life. I was crushed. Mom asked what was wrong, and I told her. Finally Dad got home from work, and he came into my room to talk to me. Dad told me it was all right because I had tried my best. He told me to keep going to the courts and I would get better and make the team next year. I told Dad I was done with basketball. I said I'd never try out for another team because it hurt too much to get cut. I was heartbroken. Dad patted me on the head and said, "We'll see son, we'll see."

I did quit playing basketball—for a whole week. Then I picked up my basketball, and with tears rolling down my cheeks, I ran out of the house dribbling, running, and crying all the way to the courts.

As I started shooting baskets, the tears dried on my cheeks and the love for the game surged back into me. I played basketball for many hours that day—nearly forgetting about dinner. I ran into the house just in time for dinner. Dad saw me with my basketball— and smiled. He knew I wasn't done with basketball. Not by a long shot.

So I went back to the courts every day. I was playing the game that I loved too much to quit even after being badly hurt. The eighth grade coach felt bad about cutting me and asked if I'd like to be the team's scorekeeper. I was so embarrassed about getting cut that I didn't want to. But again, my love for the game prevailed. So I kept score and went to all of the games. But that winter was a hollow time for me. Basketball was everything, and not being on the team left me feeling empty inside. During the next spring and summer I was at the courts a lot, and I also went by my friends' courts where they had the pick-up games and joined in. So I played as much or more basketball the spring and summer before my freshman year as I had any other year—and I played in far more pick-up games than ever before. I could clearly feel the difference.

Wouldn't you know, they had a free-throw championship for all of the eighth graders at the end of that year. Some of the guys from the team asked me if I was going to enter it. I said I didn't think so because I hadn't even made the team. They said that didn't matter because they knew I was a good shot. I entered the contest and wasn't really nervous about it. After all, I had been cut from the team, so no one expected much from me. I remember the first shot was a swisher—no rim, no backboard, just net. The next five were the same. My seventh shot bounced on the rim and off the backboard and in. That made seven in a row. Now I could feel the pressure, but still I swished the next two—having made nine in a row. I felt this was probably good enough to win, but I wanted that last shot. Maybe it would make everyone know, including me, that I wasn't quite done with basketball yet. How could I be if I could make ten out of ten free throws and beat every kid who made the basketball team from which I was cut? My tenth shot seemed in slow motion. It arced toward the rim perfectly. It was nothing but net, a swisher, and a thing of beauty. I had done it—ten out of ten free throws. They put my name up in the gym:

Free Throw Champ
Butler 10–10

I kind of wondered what my basketball coach thought about having cut the kid who made ten out of ten free throws in the free-throw contest. But I'll never know as he didn't say anything to me.

So although getting cut from the basketball team was a huge loss for me, no one was going to take this free-throw record away from me. It was perfect, and I'm guessing it stood up for quite a while—probably forever …

Chapter 3

High School—
the Beginning

In September I started high school—my freshman year. Many of my basketball buddies asked me if I was going to try out for the team. My response was I didn't think so because I didn't want to get cut again. But these guys told me that I had caught up and would make it this time. I was not convinced.

Somehow Dad found out tryouts were coming up. He asked me if I was going to try out, and I told him no; I didn't want to get cut again. Dad said that there was both an A and B freshman team, and he was sure I'd caught up with the other guys and would at least make the B team. But I insisted that I wasn't going to go out for the team. I started to cry and went running out of the house, down the sidewalk, with Dad in hot pursuit.

Dad caught me. He said that even if I didn't want to go out for myself, he asked me if I would do it for him as he had played high school basketball for Griffith too. I finally agreed, even though I was still afraid of getting cut.

The week for tryouts came, and I was very nervous. I remember all the butterflies in my stomach in the locker room as I got changed. I was so afraid that somehow I had not got caught up and would be cut. The first day of tryouts put my mind somewhat at ease. I was not only as good as the others in the fundamentals of shooting, dribbling, defense, rebounding, etc., but I also played well in our first scrimmage, which really was the key for me. Still I couldn't help being nervous as we went through tryouts. I was still afraid of getting cut in spite of knowing I had "caught up" big time. Again I survived the first two cuts, but I was afraid of the last one. Although I was almost sure I would make the B team, I wasn't positive and still had doubts.

All of the worry was for naught. When the coach posted the names of the players on the A and B teams, I was elated. I not only made it, but I was on the A team. And right from the first practice with the A team I was on the starting five. I couldn't believe it. I had not only made the team but the starting five on the A team. To think I had done this after having been cut from the eighth-grade team and missing all those practices and games. It was almost incomprehensible.

I was thrilled beyond belief. My dad was thrilled as well but not beyond belief. He always believed in me and knew I had the same passion for basketball as he had as a kid. I thanked him for pushing me to try out and for believing I had caught up. And I had learned how to stay caught up by playing in the pick-up games. I knew I would continue to do it because I loved basketball. Playing on the high school team fed my Hoosier hysteria to off-the-chart levels. This was all a part of my love for the game.

As if making the freshman team was not reward enough, the make-up of the team was great. Most of the players were kids I grew up with through elementary and junior high. But now the team included players who had gone to the catholic grade school, St. Mary's. And one of those players was my baseball friend, Marty. I not only made the team, but my friendships were also growing, especially my friendship with Marty. And to give you an idea of how much Marty and I loved basketball, we would often go to the courts and play basketball after basketball practice.

Marty and I had a lot of basketball buddies. Most were on the school teams but not all. Bill was a great friend and basketball buddy, but he was not on the team. Bill only lived a block away from me, so he and I were very close. Bill was short, but he could still play basketball. He was a good shot and he could handle (dribble) the ball well. And Bill could hold his own in the pick-up games at the courts. David (DY), Randy (RO), and Scotty were other friends who were not only basketball buddies but also were on the school teams, at least through our freshman and sophomore years.

DY lived right behind Marty and had a half-court basketball court in his backyard. There was a lot of basketball played in DY's backyard—especially pickup games, but more on that later. The one thing you should know about DY is that if you dared him to do almost anything, he would do it. One time in the winter we were hanging around the railroad tracks that were not all that far from Marty and DY's house.

We were talking about how sometimes your tongue would stick to steel when it was cold. Someone dared DY to lick the railroad tracks. DY hesitated, and then he knelt down and licked the track and his tongue did in fact stick. We thought he was kidding, and we told him to get up. He couldn't as his tongue was stuck, but good. Then someone said they thought they heard a train coming, to which DY started moaning and crying. We listened and didn't hear anything. Someone said in the movies sometimes they would put their ear on the track to better hear if a train was coming. I said no way, we already had DY with his tongue stuck so all we needed was for someone else to get their ear stuck. We knew we had to get DY's tongue off, but we had no idea what to do. Finally, I said I would go and get DY's mom. When I got to DY's house, his mom was not happy when I told her. She got a glass of water, and she and I kind of marched off to the railroad tracks. She had a hold of my arm—kind of like it was my fault. When we got there, everyone got back as DY's mom gave everyone the evil eye and then poured the water onto DY's tongue, which freed him. She asked what happened, and DY said, "They dared me, Mom." And then she grabbed DY's arm and marched him home.

As far as basketball goes, it's too bad someone hadn't dared DY to be a great basketball player because he was close—very good but not great. He was more a deliberate type of player. He handled the ball well with both hands and had a good shot, but mostly from the outside as he did not often go to the basket. He made the freshman high school team but was cut in tryouts for junior varsity his sophomore year.

Randy (RO) was a more athletic player than DY. RO was fast, could go to the basket, and played good defense. RO was on the high school team through his junior year but was cut our senior year.

Scotty was one of those guys who matured early and was big for his age. As a freshman player he dominated and ultimately was up on the varsity squad as a reserve. But Scotty was one of those guys who peaked too early. He was cut in tryouts his sophomore year.

Our freshman team was unremarkable at best. Although our group of boys had been consistent winners through sixth, seventh, and eighth grade, something had changed. We were the same boys, but we didn't play with the same passion. Oh, we won some games, but not that many. As for me, I was having a decent season, scoring my share of points, etc. But as a forward, if the point guard passed the ball to the other side on offense, I was not directly involved in the play. Maybe it was my imagination, but the play seemed to flow to the other side of the court a majority of the time. I felt left out, so I started concentrating on something else that kept me involved in the game: rebounding. I soon realized I did not have to have the ball passed to me to be a part of the offense. I could get under the basket and position myself for rebounds. Once I started doing this, my rebounding improved dramatically, and I quickly became one of the better rebounders on the team. The more I rebounded, the more I jumped. And the more I jumped, the higher I jumped. The higher you jumped, the more rebounds you got. And you score more points as well by getting rebounds under the offensive basket.

With the season two-thirds over, my season came to an abrupt halt. During one of the games I was involved in a fast break, and as we approached our basket, the pass to me was too far forward, headed out of bounds under the basket. I was running full speed as I jumped and tried to throw the ball back in bounds. My right foot slammed into the brick stage behind the basket just below the padded area.

My foot hurt like mad, but I kept playing. At the end of the game, I got an offensive rebound right under our basket. As I was going up for an easy basket, I tried to push off my right foot but I couldn't, which resulted in a missed shot as the horn sounded the end of the game. This also turned out to be the end of my freshman basketball season as I had broken my big toe joint. In the locker room my foot was so swelled after the game, I could not get my shoe off. The next day's x-rays confirmed the break, and accordingly, my doctor confirmed the end of my basketball season as well.

After a couple of months of taking it easy, I was back to the basketball courts in the spring. And who was also at the basketball courts nearly every day with me? Marty. So Marty and I kind of hung out at the courts when we weren't playing Babe Ruth baseball. Marty and I normally would play at the public courts near my house, but we also played at St. Mary's courts near Marty's house. We also played at our friend DY's house. We played shooting games (horse, twenty-one, around-the-world), we played one-on-one, but mostly we played in pick-up games—often with older kids. Marty and I were players and could hold our own with most anybody—even the better players. It surely wasn't as easy to hold your own with the better players. But we had game, and the tough play with the better players only made us better. During the spring, summer, and fall, Marty and I would spend all day at the courts, go home for supper, and then go back to the courts and play until 10:00 or when the lights would go out—sometime between 9:00 and 10:00. We didn't do this every day but probably four to five days a week. To say that we spent hundreds of hours on the basketball courts throughout our high school years was easily an understatement.

To give you an idea of what kind of friends Marty and I were, it helps to understand some of our antics from our second year of Babe Ruth baseball when we were fourteen. Marty was a pitcher and I was a catcher on our team, the Cubs. Pitchers and catchers have a unique role and relationship on a baseball team. The catcher gives the pitcher signals that tell the pitcher what pitch to throw. And of course there are those pitcher/catcher conferences on the mound. Well, when the pitcher and catcher are two fourteen-year-old boys who are good friends, the role of pitcher and catcher takes on a different slant.

As a catcher, I would be giving pitch signals to Marty, and all of a sudden I would give him the finger and he would start laughing. And when either of us saw a good-looking girl in the stands, we would call a conference and I'd go out to the mound and point the girl out to Marty or he would do the same for me. The umpires never knew exactly what was going on with us, but they knew it was more than just baseball.

I'll never forget the time in a game when a guy came up to bat that neither I nor Marty liked. Marty was pitching so I went through my signs and then touched the side of my head—jokingly indicating a bean ball. I thought Marty would laugh. But no, Marty didn't laugh. He hauled off and threw a fast ball at the guy. The guy hit the dirt as the ball sailed over him. I called time-out and went out to the mound and told Marty that I was just kidding around and when I touched the side of my head it was a joke and that he shouldn't really throw at the guy. Marty said okay. So I went back and went through my signs, and I again touched the side of my head. So does Marty laugh? No, he throws at this guy again, and this time he almost hits him. At that point the umpire had caught on to what we were doing, and he threw us both out of the game. When we were in the dugout, after getting chewed out by our manager, I asked Marty what he was thinking about. He said he didn't like the guy, and after I had signaled bean ball, he said he decided he was going to try to plunk him. I think that was the last time I signaled bean ball, but we sure had fun with the crazy signals and conferences on the mound.

In another game where Marty was pitching and I was catching, it was in the last inning with two outs and a man on second with the game tied. The batter hit a sharp single to left. Our left fielder charged the ball and made a perfect throw to me at home. We had the guy dead to rights as he was trying to score the winning run from second, so I was blocking the plate as catchers sometimes do. This guy lowered his shoulder and bowled me over, and we both went tumbling. He landed on top of me and across me as I came to rest on my side. The ball just barely dribbled out of my mitt, so I quickly scooped it back in, but this guy on top of me saw it, as had their whole team as I was facing their dugout. The umpire did not see the ball come out because he was behind me and the kid across me blocked his view. The umpire called him out, and a frenzy ensued as the other team was screaming that I had dropped the ball. Their coach was beside himself. Finally the umpire asked me if I dropped the ball, and I said no. If the umpire didn't see it, I wasn't going to tell him. Marty took me aside and said he saw me drop the ball. I said I didn't care; I wasn't going to fess up. Then my coach took me aside and asked me and again and I said no. He told me to tell the truth, and I said I didn't want to. He said I had to, so I finally gave in and told the ump I dropped the ball. The umpire called him safe, and we lost the game.

I told Marty I was sorry I dropped the ball and lost the game. He said, "That's okay because the next time that kid comes to bat when I'm pitching, I'm going to plunk him and then we'll be even. That'll teach him to knock over my catcher and best friend."

I said, "Thanks, Marty. That makes me feel better. I kind of like it when you plunk a guy for a good reason."

And you know later that day, I knew what I should have done. I should have told the umpire that after I scooped up the ball I tagged the guy who was lying on top of me. And I was on top of the plate, so likely he hadn't touched it. The ump wouldn't have seen that either. I told Marty about that, and he said, "Forget about it. You can only lie so much to an umpire. They might throw you out of the whole league." I told Marty maybe I should try this out on our coach. But Marty finally convinced me to let it go. What's done is done. But I still kind of wondered and started thinking maybe I really had touched him with my glove after scooping the ball back into my mitt …

Chapter 4

Junior Varsity

With the fall of my sophomore year came the basketball tryouts, with Marty and me in the middle of it. Although I knew my skills had grown as much or more than the other players on the team, I still had some nagging doubts as I hadn't finished my freshman year on the team because of my broken toe. The tryouts for junior varsity (JV) confirmed my improved abilities, as did the final list of names on the JV roster. Both Marty and I made the team. I was a starting forward, and Marty was a sub (substitute). The other starters were Lenny (point guard), Pete (shooting guard), Jim (center), and Tom (forward). And once again, our team was unremarkable, finishing with a record of six wins and twelve losses. We had good players, but we didn't seem able to click as a team.

But in spite of the team struggling, me, Marty, and all of our other teammates all improved.

One game stood out in particular for me. It was against Hammond Tech at Tech's school. Tech had been having problems in their school with pretty big fights almost race riots (between whites and Hispanics) breaking out among the students. There was some concern about playing there given the tense atmosphere in the school. The concern was enough that they had a police car accompany our player bus to and from the school.

As our game progressed, I was being guarded by a Hispanic guy who was constantly fouling me. Some of these fouls were called by the refs but many were not, and I had just about had enough when I went up for a jump shot and this kid clawed me in the face. A foul was called but I still had the ball.

I slammed it down, walked up to the kid who fouled me, and poked him in the chest and said, "I don't mind getting fouled, but don't claw me in the face."

Pete jumped in between me and this guy and kept saying, "Cool it, Rab, just cool it." (My basketball nickname had become Rab which was short for rabbit—because I could jump so high.)

The referees jumped in between us as well and were pushing me away from this kid. Then my coach called time-out. I didn't think it was a big deal. All I had done was poke the kid in the chest after he clawed me in the face. I didn't understand why everyone was getting so excited. Well, I was about to find out how big a deal this was …

As I went to the sidelines, I saw our (Griffith's) vice principal come down on the floor. He went up to me in our huddle and told me that I had to go apologize to the kid I had challenged (poked in the chest) and shake his hand. I said that guy should apologize to me because he clawed me in the face. The vice principal wanted to hear none of that and told me that if I didn't apologize and shake the kid's hand, I was going to be expelled from school. Obviously, they were concerned about some kind of riot breaking out.

So against my better judgment, I went to the kid, said I was sorry, and shook his hand. I made my free throws, and coincidently or not, the kid pretty much quit fouling me. My actions must have been okay because there were no fights or riots and I did not get expelled from school. That was the end of the excitement in that game.

Chapter 5

Varsity

During my sophomore year, I learned how good I was at rebounding. I was a good jumper and had good hands, so I could rebound with one hand, which got me higher than most of the other taller kids under the basket. I also learned the importance of rebounding position and to anticipate my teammates' shots in order to position myself for rebounds. I became a good rebounder, which was important to our success as a team. The off-season between my sophomore and junior years was more of the same—endless hours at the basketball courts day after day after day.

The next fall Marty and I made the varsity basketball team as juniors. I was the seventh man and got a fair amount of playing time, and Marty was also a reserve—but played less. Our varsity team was decent—accumulating a record slightly better than five hundred. At the end of the season, Griffith drew a tough Merrillville team in the second game of the state tournament sectionals. The game was hard fought, very close, and I had not played the entire game when, with two minutes to go, our center fouled out.

The center was six foot three whereas I was only five foot eleven, but regardless, the coach put me in for the rest of the game as center. With ten seconds to go in the game, I got an offensive rebound under the basket and went up for the shot. I was fouled and had two free throws with my team trailing by two points. The Merrillville coach called time out to try to ice me.

In the huddle my coach kept saying over and over, "You've got to make them, Butler—you've got to make them."

I felt like asking him if I could go take a couple of practice free throws because I had hardly played and had taken no shots. Finally, the horn sounded, and I walked up to the free-throw line. Everyone lined up for the free throws, and the ref gave me the ball. My heart was pounding, and I tried to block out all the screaming in the stands from a packed crowd. Although I had been ten for ten in the free-throw contest, the question now was could I be two for two in the state tournament with the game and the rest of the season all on the line. This was what I dreamed of—making a last-minute shot to save the big game.

I thought of being at the courts and took a deep breath. My first shot swished through the basket. I knew I could do it. My second shot was nothing but net. I had made the two biggest shots of my basketball career. This tied the game, and it went into overtime. Everyone was patting me on the back in the huddle— even the coach—saying, "Way to go, Rab, way to go." (And the coach never called me Rab, but he did that time.) But my stardom was short-lived as Merrillville commenced to blow us out in the overtime. Exactly what caused the blowout was unclear, but the fact that I was playing out of position as center surely didn't help. I was a good rebounder, but I had trouble going back up and shooting after my offensive rebounds under the basket. Although I was becoming a very good jumper, many of my rebounds were one handed, and I only controlled the ball with two hands as I brought the ball down. So for me to shoot, I had to bring the ball back up through the taller guys under the basket, and they would stuff me, blocking my shot.

This issue continued to plague me the following year as well, and the coach was never able to come up with good solutions for me. Now, in retrospect, I think I should have jumped back or forward as I went up to draw contact, creating a foul. And this was not a small issue for me as I often would tip offensive rebounds rather than bring them down and get trapped by the taller defensive players. And tip-ins are a low-percentage shot as they are difficult to make, whereas bringing down the rebound and creating fouls would have given me more rebounds and points from the free-throw line.

Again, the off season was characterized by playing as much basketball at the courts as I could between my summer job (a lifeguard at a local country club) and my girlfriends and dates. And speaking of being a lifeguard, it was the greatest job in the world for a sixteen-year-old guy. Basically you were being paid for getting a suntan and also to meet girls. For some reason, many girls were attracted to lifeguards. They liked to flirt with us, so it was easy getting dates with some good-looking babes.

Also during the summer word came down that any basketball player who did not play football in the fall had to run cross-country if they wanted to be on the basketball team. Well, I didn't play football so I had to run cross-country—two miles for time.

Although I was a fast runner, I didn't like running or track, so I didn't really want to run cross-country. But I had little choice. Our basketball coach was also the cross-country coach. Marty was a good cross-country runner, and he encouraged me to start training early in the summer before the actual practices started. So I went out for a run with Marty and some of the other runners on the team. I had a lot of trouble keeping up with these guys, so I dropped out and decided any advance running would be on my own. I did go for a few runs before formal practices started, but they were pretty short and not nearly enough. When the actual practices started, I again had similar trouble with the training runs—trouble keeping up. So I did the best I could but basically dogged the practices (did as little as I could to get by).

Finally just before the meets were about to start, they had a time trial. This was a two-mile run that the coach timed to simulate a cross country meet. On the way to the time trials the other runners were moaning and groaning—saying it was going to be horrible. I knew I had run two miles before, so I laughed and said, "It can't be that bad," and they said, "You wait, you wait." And unfortunately they were right—it was horrible. The first mile wasn't too bad, but the second mile was a killer. I had gotten side aches before from running but nothing like this. The last half mile felt like five miles. I finished dead last with a time of twelve minutes and forty-five seconds. I also threw up after the race.

Now I knew what running a two-mile race was all about. I decided I had better try taking this whole thing more seriously. So I actually ran harder during practices, but none of this was easy, fun, or nearly enough to make me competitive. In the first meet I ran a twelve thirty-eight. I wasn't dead last but close and nowhere near to the middle of the finishers.

The next couple of meets were more of the same. And then to add insult to injury, they added an eighth grader to our team who was some kind of a phenom. Well, I wasn't a good cross-country runner, but I sure didn't want this kid to beat me. At the next meet I made sure I was ahead of this kid until the last half mile as once again I got a big side ache and slowed down.

But of course, the kid didn't. As the eighth grader passed me, I was tempted to trip him but I didn't. The good news was I had run my fastest time. The bad news was I was once again dead last on our team and was even beaten by an eighth-grader.

Well, finally my last meet was approaching. I wanted to run in the elevens (under twelve minutes), which would at least be somewhat respectable. But my experience told me no matter how much I paced myself; I would still get a side ache and slow down toward the end of the race. So I came up with what I thought was a brilliant strategy—go out fast and hang on. I told my buddies about my new strategy.

They said, "No way—do not do that—bad idea. Don't do it, Rab, don't do it!" But I had made up my mind, and bad plan or not, I was going to give it a shot.

So as the gun went off for this last meet, I took off with the lead pack in the race. I was up with the front-runners. My split time at the mile mark was just over five minutes—a blistering pace that I was bound to pay for. My buddy Marty saw me at the split and said, "Rick, what are you doing up here?"

I said, "New strategy."

And Marty shook his head and said, "Oh no."

Well, you can kind of guess what happened. I got the mother of all side aches, and I slowed way down. It seemed like everyone in the world was passing me. Compared to the other runners, it looked like I was moon walking. But my buddies were encouraging me, saying, "Way to go, Rab—don't stop." Although I wanted to stop so bad I could taste it, I kept on. And finally I saw the finish line, and my buddies were rooting me on: "11:30, 11:45 you're going to make it." And I did, barely, with an 11:58. I threw up to end my cross-country career. On the way home after the meet my buddies were congratulating me and laughing. I wasn't laughing because I was still hurting. There were two good things about the end of cross-country. First of all the agony of running two miles for time was over. But more importantly, our senior year of basketball was about to begin. I just hoped my senior year on the basketball team would make it all worthwhile. And as it turned out it did—in spades …

Ironically, years later when I was in my mid-thirties I was training for my third marathon (26.2 miles for time). I was in the best shape of my life, and I had started running intervals on the Apple Valley High School track. One day I was thinking and decided I could actually run two miles in under twelve minutes given the shape I was in. I took many deep breaths and took off. After six laps (one and one half miles) I started hurting, but it wasn't the mother of all side aches and I was well ahead of the pace I needed. I knew I could gut it out and make it. So I got about half way through that seventh lap and it was hurting more, so I just stopped. Although I could have done it, it wasn't worth it. And I never ran on that track again.

Marty and I continued playing at the courts, and now we were undoubtedly some of the best guys out there. We not only could play with anyone, but we were better than almost all the other guys. As basketball season approached, there was no doubt that we were ready. At five foot eleven I was a small forward, but I played big and was a good rebounder. Marty had grown a bunch and now was approaching six foot four, and he was a good leaper as well. And Marty's feet had grown to a size sixteen, so he was known as Foot. Well, Foot had big hands, so at six foot four he could palm the ball and dunk. I couldn't palm the ball, so only with a lot of sticky stuff on my hand could I dunk. Marty and I would practice our jumping at the courts. One thing we did was practice "putting the lid on," which was a basketball term for jamming a rebound back into the basket with one hand as it came off the rim. We'd take turns with one guy shooting the ball off the backboard or rim as the other guy came running in and soared above the rim for the jam. It was a thing of beauty when it worked, but mostly it didn't as the timing and shot had to be just right. But clearly Marty and I were playing above the rim, and together we were a rebounding force to be reckoned with.

In retrospect probably one of the best things that happened to me in my early years of playing basketball was getting cut off the eighth grade team. Although it was devastating at the time, it caused me to kind of back up and regroup. I knew what the problem was—I hadn't played in nearly enough pick-up games. Although I was a good shot (ten out of ten free throws), a good dribbler with both hands, and could do all the drills, lay-ins, etc., as good or better than any of the others, I wasn't good at scrimmaging—the pick-up games. After getting cut, I joined in those pick-up games, especially with Marty's encouragement. And it wasn't long before I was playing very well as I not only had the skills but also had practice in applying them. I learned a couple of lessons from this. I learned that you can't and shouldn't quit the things that you love. And I learned that getting knocked down was okay if you learned from it and got back up. In fact, as it turned out our whole team got back up for our senior year big time …

Chapter 6

Best Season Ever: Twenty and Four

I looked forward to basketball tryouts my senior year. Given that I was seventh man on varsity my junior year, there seemed no question that I would make the team and likely be a starter. Marty, however, would tell you that until the final cut-list was posted, you never knew for sure who would make the team. But Marty's growth and improvement clearly made him a potential starter as well. Both Marty and I loved to play basketball, so tryouts and practice were fun, except for maybe the wind sprints at the end of each practice.

Finally the first day of senior year tryouts arrived. I remember my heart beating and the feeling of joy as we went in for our first lay-ups. After that first scrimmage at the end of the first day of tryouts I knew Marty and I were locks to make the team and likely as starters. Marty was not so sure. I told him we were locked in—so just play hard and enjoy the ride.

Ironically, after the final tryouts and cut lists, only two of the twelve players remained from the eighth-grade team grade team that I couldn't make—Pete and Lenny. All the rest had been cut somewhere along the way. Once we had made the team, Marty and I talked about how it felt to be seniors on our last high school team. It was kind of like this was our team. As starters we really wanted to play well, as this was our goal from the first tryout our freshman year—to become varsity starters.

Our team consisted of twelve guys—mostly juniors and seniors. However, it was pretty much our seniors' team because four of the five starters were seniors. Marty became the starting center, and I became a starting forward. The other seniors on the starting five were Lenny (Skinner) as our point guard and Pete (Nisky) as our shooting guard. One junior started as the baseline forward—Kerry. We weren't sure how good we were, but we were about to find out ...

It's funny because almost all of us had nicknames, Lenny (a.k.a., Skinner) was our point guard. He was about five foot ten and was skinny as a rail and very fast. I never was quite sure where his nickname came from. I thought it had something to do with how skinny he was. Later I was told that he got that nickname playing pickup games with some of the older kids who got frustrated with Lenny stealing the ball all the time. He was so fast and skinny he kind of skinned the ball away from you, hence the nickname Skinner. Anyway, he would lead us flying down the court on fast breaks. He handled the ball well and could go either to his left or right, although he was a natural left hander. When he pulled up for a jump shot, he would square up and plant both of his feet next to each other for his jumper, which normally would come from the top of the key or near the free throw line. Lenny drove to the basket frequently using his speed and agility. He also would end up on the floor under the basket quite often following his drives. But he always managed to get that skinny body up and go back for more. There was no quit in Lenny. Skinner would get fifteen or so points per game and a number of assists. And as you might have guessed,

Skinner usually got a couple of steals each game as well.

Pete (a.k.a., Nisky) was the off-guard or shooting guard. Pete's last name ended in "nisky" thus the nickname Nisky—not quite rocket science. Pete too was a lefty and was our best and purest shooter. He played a wing in our one-three-one offense. Pete had a smooth, great shot. His heydays were against a zone defense. We'd move the ball around the perimeter, and if Pete had the slightest opening—bam, nothing but net. He seldom missed an open jumper. He also seldom drove to the basket as he only could go to his left. But Pete would knock down a few jumpers each game—usually scoring between five and ten points. Pete was our all-American boy. He was good looking (a lot like Rob Lowe), was on the student council, had a great personality, and was our homecoming king our senior year and one of our class officers. Pete and I were very good friends, having gone to school together since kindergarten. We'd been basketball teammates from the fifth grade, continuing through high school. Pete and I also walked to school together all four years of high school.

Marty (a.k.a., Foot) was six foot four and was also a lefty. With size sixteen and a half shoes, the most important thing you should know about Marty's development as a basketball player was that he finally grew into his feet between his junior and senior year. He could jump and clearly was a force to be reckoned with under the basket. He was a great rebounder, and he blocked a whole bunch of shots on defense. When someone from the other team drove to the basket, they usually had Marty to contend with, who would contest or block their shots. He also ran the floor well—both ways. He too could only go to his left, but with his height, long arms, and jumping ability, he could go up as well and even dunk the ball. He played above the rim and cleaned up the offensive boards, scoring most of his points from the paint or the baseline—normally ten to fifteen points per game with a similar number of rebounds. Up until our senior year, I could always beat Marty in one-on-one basketball games as I was faster and more athletic. But all that changed when the Foot grew into his feet. He could take me or pretty much anyone on our team in one on one. But mostly Marty and I did not play each other in one on one because we were best friends. And best friends help each other. They don't beat each other.

Kerry was a junior. He was six foot three, right handed, and played power forward on the baseline. Kerry had a very good turn around fade-away jump shot that was hard to block. He had a soft shot and was our scoring machine. Kerry was a big guy and took up a lot of space under the boards. His bread and butter were his ten-foot turn-around fade-away jumpers. He made a ton of them. His size made him a good rebounder—especially on offense. He was extremely smart but was pretty much an independent thinker—kind of in a league of his own. And yet he still was a team player—we all were. But on offense, he was the man—scoring twenty-five-plus points per game.

Our gym was standard for the 1960s. The lower level had pull out bleachers that were normally left folded up to expand the gym and allow play at side baskets. There were also bleachers in the balcony that were pulled out for games only. We had pep rallies the afternoon before each basketball game (Fridays for weekend games.) These were during the school day, so the whole senior high school attended. Usually the principal, assistant principal, or basketball coach would say some words about the importance of the upcoming game. Then our cheerleaders would lead the entire school through deafening cheers to stir everyone into a fevered frenzy. Our varsity team sat up front, and sometimes they would have us stand up or go out in front for them to cheer us on for encouragement and hopefully victory.

Our cheerleaders, led by Captain Wendy, were cute, athletic, and basically a bundle of energy. They led the frenzied cheers from our fans. And make no mistake about it, our team could definitely hear and feel this support on the basketball court. It made us tingle with excitement.

Cheerleaders: Judy, Wendy (captain), Lana (panther), Chris, and Janet

To give you a sense of the importance of high school basketball in the area, our local daily paper, the *Hammond Times*, printed stories and box scores for each of the local high school games. They often ran game pictures of us as well. And if print media wasn't enough, our local radio stations broadcast many of our games live.

First Game

This was a dream come true for many of us on that team—especially the seniors. We had worked so hard for so long, and now we were the guys. I remember in the locker room before the game Coach gave us his pep talk, and you could have heard a pin drop. He closed these talks with words of encouragement, telling us this was our game, the beginning of our season. And as we waited for our team to be announced, our hearts were pounding with pride, excitement, and the love of the game. It was surging inside of us as we ran out onto the court with the crowd roaring. We always started our warm-ups by going out and touching the rim or the net. We felt as if we were soaring in that first jump as many of us were high above the rim. Our warm-up drills were the typical lay-in kind of stuff, but we put effort into them. So by game time we would be breaking a sweat. Then the coach would indicate who was starting by tugging on each starter's warm-up for us to take them off to get ready to play. What a feeling of pride as he tugged on our jerseys. And he not only tugged on the starter's jerseys but also on each substitute player's jersey as he put them into the game. In essence, each tug meant it was game-time. Get in there and play.

Every time he tugged on my jersey, especially to start, it reminded me of how I had worked so hard and focused my life to reach this pinnacle. Basketball was my life. Each tug was a little gesture that meant absolutely everything to me. And I was fortunate because I got starting tugs for almost every game that joyous season for the Griffith Panthers varsity basketball team—a dream come true.

The first game was against Whiting High School. And I remember that first tip Marty went way up and tapped the ball back to Lenny. Lenny then led us down the floor for the first of many, many times that season. We (Griffith) came out running with our fast-breaking offense. As one of the forwards or center would get the defensive rebound, they would make an outlet pass to one of the guards, who most often was Lenny, who would start the fast break, taking the ball down the center of the court. The rebounder would fill one of the fast-break lanes, with a forward or guard filling the other side. The result was the guard with the ball was in the middle and there were two wing men on each side leading the fast break. If the guard with the ball was not stopped, he would go to the basket and the wing men would rebound. But usually the guard with the ball would be defended and would stop at the free-throw line and look for a pass to either of the wing men, who were streaking down their sides for a potential lay-in. If neither wing man was open then one of the trailing players would possibly be open. But if not, the ball would go back out to the point and ultimately to Lenny, who would set up the offense. The offense was a one-three-one and involved weak side picks and rolls. On defense we (Griffith) would play mostly a match-up zone or a sagging man to man.

We went out to an early lead against Whiting and never looked back as we won eighty-two to sixty-two. I had a good game with sixteen points and ten rebounds. My free throw percentage was not that good as I only made four of eight free throws. In fact the whole team shot poorly at the free throw line. But it mattered little as we coasted to a twenty-point victory with Marty and Lenny scoring double figures as well. This first victory felt good, and little did we know that it was the beginning of our glorious ride through Hoosier hysteria and Griffith basketball history.

Still our coach was concerned about our free throws. We shot free throws well in practice but missed far too many in the game. The difference, Coach told us, was we were shooting them in games when we were tired and winded, whereas in practice we shot them at the end of practice but before our wind sprints.

He changed that, and we practiced our free throws after wind sprints when good and tired. At first we had trouble similar to what we'd had in the game, but with practice we got better.

————

The next couple of games against Gavit and Portage had similar outcomes as we scored eighty-plus points and won by at least twenty. I scored six points and fifteen points respectively in those victories and again had double-digit rebounds along with the Foot. And again, Kerry and Skinner led our scoring.

————

The next two games we lost to Highland and Gary Edison. Coincidently or otherwise, I had the flu and played very little in these (single-digit) losses. I remember playing just before the end of the half in the Gary Edison game. I felt awful, got sick, and was throwing up in the locker room during halftime.

————

The last game before the holiday tournament we regained our stride, beating Hammond Tech by six points.

By this point in the season the starting five had pretty much fallen into their roles on the team. Our starting five varied a little, but mostly the starters were seniors Lenny, Pete, Marty, and me, plus Kerry, who was a junior.

I was five foot eleven and played small forward. I could jump, so I played big like Marty—above the rim. I was a good defensive player and rebounder—almost as good as Marty. When Marty or I went up for the ball, look out. We would rip the ball off the boards as if we owned it. In most games we did own the boards, especially on defense. I was a righty but could go either to my left or to the right. I wasn't as pure of a shooter as Pete, but I was a good shot. I could go to the basket and had a spin dribble where I changed hands and direction, pivoting 360 degrees. I would practice that move with Marty and called it my Earl the Pearl Monroe move. Earl the Pearl was an NBA player who pretty much had patented that move. I also had a turn-around fade-away bank shot off the backboard that I would shoot from the wing just outside the paint. I called it my Wilt the Stilt shot. Wilt the Stilt Chamberlin (one of the all-time great NBA players) had patented that move. I used my Earl the Pearl move in games sometimes but never my Wilt the Stilt shot as it was strictly for fun.

But mostly I was a rebounder. I would tear down defensive rebounds, hit Lenny in stride on fast breaks, and then come flying down to fill the lane. I was also pretty much a role player. I knew my job was to feed Kerry, rebound, and play good defense. I would get around ten points a game, somewhere between ten and fifteen rebounds, and a ton of assists to Kerry.

As mentioned before, in practice Marty or I would shoot the ball off the backboard as the other would run and jump up, trying to jam the ball in the basket for a dunk. It seldom worked and never like it did in our last game before the holiday tournament

Early in this game Lenny was shooting a free-throw, and I was lined up on the left side of the free-throw lane. As Lenny shot the ball, I crouched down and was ready. As the ball approached the basket, I took one step and jumped with my right hand rising up above the rim nearly to my elbow. The shot came off the back of the rim straight back over the basket right into my hand. I guided the ball down into the basket for the first ever jam in Griffith basketball history.

This was a quick move that surprised everyone, including me and the refs. It was as if the ball was in slow motion as it came off the rim and nestled into my hand. And normally Marty or I would have tried to jam it with authority. But that's probably why we missed so many jams. Maybe I guided it instead of jamming it because I didn't want to miss the basket and be accused of hot dogging it. In any event, the startled ref hesitated, possibly wondering how that could have happened without me being in the lane too early, raised two fingers, and put them down, indicating a two-point basket. During the next time-out my buddies came up to me and said, "Way to go, Rab, you got a jam." The coach never said a word but was as surprised as anyone.

———

The holiday tournament was played just before Christmas, and we had clearly hit our stride. We beat Crown Point sixty-seven to fifty-four and avenged our loss to Highland by beating them in the championship game seventy-seven to sixty-seven. Although we played great in that tournament, the tournament was remembered most for the snow storm that dumped twelve inches of snow during the tournament finals.

The Highland game may have been my best game of the year, scoring ten points and pulling down a whopping seventeen rebounds. My cousin Pam was a cheerleader for Highland. She said the talk at their school was that it wasn't Kerry or Lenny that beat them; it was Marty and Rick who were all over the court.

In the Crown Point game I pretty much shut down their leading scorer. This guy was totally ambidextrous.

He would dribble down the right side of the court and stop and knock down twenty-foot jumpers with his right hand, then do the same thing down the left side and knock down the same twenty-foot jumpers with his left hand. That was his game—drive to the baseline and fire up twenty-foot jumpers. But I knew his game, and I was all over him as he went up for his shots. I blocked a few, swatting one out of bounds, and clearly disrupted his game. Crown Point was ranked number nine in the whole state of Indiana (small and big schools alike) when we beat them.

———

Griffith Nips Highland Bid In 72-67 Win

Times Sports Writer

CROWN POINT—Moon - faced Harold (Red) M a c k couldn't contain himself as his delirious players shouted and jigged on the sidelines.

Exchanging shouts and slapping backs, Mack made his way to Kerry Pickett shortly after Griffith High School defeated Highland, 72-67, to win t h e Crown Point Holiday Basketball Tournament h e r e Wednesday night.

Pickett, a f r e c k l e d, redthatched junior, s c o r e d 27 points before fouling out late in the fourth period to propel the Panthers' precious triumph.

HEAD back and f i s t s clenched, Pickett shouted as if to some celestial being. "We're number one, we're n u m b e r one."

Moments earlier, Pickett had been named most v a l u a b l e player of this year's two - day classic but the scrappy 6-foot-3 forward chose to exchange repartee with his teammates rather than bathe in his laurels.

"How do you feel?" M a c k asked, referring to Pickett's award.

"We're number one," c r i e d Pickett. "We're number one."

GRIFFITH'S victory was a dramatic climax to this year's Crown Point tournament.

Lightly regarded despite its 4-2 pre-tourney record, Griffith reached the winner's circle with back-to-back upsets, dumping Crown Point, 67-54 on Tuesday before taming Highland, a team that had whipped the Panthers by nine points earlier in the season.

Randy Sheets, head coach of the losing Trojans, appeared dazed while searching for his players during post-game ceremonies.

The Trojans, whose lone lead lasted 37 seconds in the second period, had scrambled.

"I GUESS my ball players are dressing," S h e e t s said meekly. "I guess I'd better go round them up."

points, was a thorn in the Panthers throughout, hitting incessantly on shots as far out as 35 feet.

In the final period, T a u b e r turned two steals into scores and led a Trojan assault that shaved Griffith's c o m m a n d from 64-51 to 65-61 within four minutes.

Crown Point barely escaped its second defeat in as many nights before finally s o l v i n g Merrillville in the opener.

Merrillville rolled to a 15-8 first-period cushion but the Bulldogs rallied to tie it at 29-29 at intermission.

DOWN by seven points (44-37) into the final lap, Crown Point trimmed its deficit to 49-48 before Cary Stump's three - point play with 1:47 left to put the Bulldogs ahead to stay.

Stump paced the Bulldogs with 14 points while Terry Pats tallied 12, Jack Pettit meshed 11 and Jeff Akers 10 in a balanced scoring attack.

Three players in double figures for Merrillville were Rick Crnovich (13), Wally Alen (11) and Wayne Svetanoff (11).

Merrillville (53)				Crown Point (55)			
	FG	FT	P		FG	FT	P
Hill	3	3-3	5	Stump	5	4-6	14
Crnovich	3	7-8	13	Pats	4	4-4	12
Alen	4	3-4	11	Germash	1	0-0	2
Lester	1	0-1	4	Akers	3	4-6	10
Sorotic	1	1-2	8	Carley	2	1-3	7
Svetanoff	4	3-3	11	Pettit	4	3-5	11
Totals	20	13-17	53	Totals	18	19-23	55

SCORE BY QUARTERS

Merrillville	15	14	15	9	—53
Crown Point	8	21	11	15	—55

Total Fouls: Merrillville 15, Crown Point 11.
Fouled Out: None.
Officials: Beckley and Alvarez.

Highland (67)				Griffith (72)			
	FG	FT	P		FG	FT	P
Boyd	3	2-3	8	Barber	7	4-5	18
LaBreg'r	2	1-2	5	Pickett	11	5-7	27
Gray	1	3-5	5	Lammons	4	0-1	8
Tauber	10	14-18	34	Zarnoth	2	0-1	4
Cresson	3	0-0	6	Kernisky	1	2-3	4
Austin	1	0-0	2	Cassidy	4	1-2	9
Smites	0	0-1	0	Schottnow	1	0-0	2
Totals	22	23-30	67	Totals	31	14-19	72

SCORE BY QUARTERS

Highland					—67
Griffith					—72

Total Fouls: Highland 16, Griffith 22.
Fouled Out: Pickett, Zarnoth, Kernisky, Boyd, Lammons.
Officials: Patty and Cox.
Technical Fouls: Highland, Grimm.

Rick Butler gets a break-away lay-up in the Holiday Tourney as Griffith beat the number nine ranked Crown Point. This was one of Rick's best games of the year

Our winning streak continued with eight more wins following the holiday tournament, making it eleven in a row. This constituted the longest winning streak in the history of Griffith basketball. One of the highlights was against Lowell. Griffith was winning fifty-five to thirty at halftime. Coach put in the subs, and by the end of the third quarter we were ahead eighty to fifty. So coach decided to put the starting five back in to go for one hundred points, which had never been reached by a Griffith team. Well, we didn't score one hundred, but we did end up with ninety-five, a school record.

Another highlight during that stretch of victories came in a home game against East Gary. We were ahead by twenty-five points with a couple of minutes to go when Coach called time-out. He wanted Marty to dunk the ball on a break-away, which had never been done before by Griffith. Coach told us, "When East Gary shoots, everyone crash the boards except Marty. He'll be hanging around at half court and will take off down the court for an outlet pass and his dunk."

The first few times it didn't work—but the next time I grabbed the rebound and hit Marty in stride. The Foot went up and jammed home the basket with a dunk. The Griffith crowd went wild—absolutely bonkers. The other coach did not appreciate Coach's antics, but the Griffith crowd sure did. They loved it as our team continued to make unparalleled basketball history for our small school in our little Hoosier town. And make no mistake this not only was basketball history for Griffith—it was town history as basketball defined who we were.

Marty and I had an unusual thing occur during our game against Hammond Noll. We were on offense, and one of our guards shot the ball. Marty and I were under the basket— Marty on the left, and I was on the right. The rebound came off toward me and I tipped the ball. The tip went too far and off to Marty, who tipped the ball, but again too far and over to me. This continued back and forth three times as Marty and I had excellent position with the defense blocked out. Finally one of the defenders had seen enough of this and hammered me—and I ended up making two free throws. This was rebounding dominance at its best.

At the end of the season, Coach made the comment about this team being one of the best rebounding and shot-blocking teams he ever had. As for rebounding, Marty and I were a huge part of this. As for shot blocking, Marty was our best by far. With his height, long arms, and leaping ability, he blocked a ton of shots, often in spectacular fashion—swatting the ball often all the way out of bounds and sometimes even up into the crowd. The teams we played against thought twice about going to the basket against us because they knew who would be there—the Foot.

The game against our archrival, Calumet, was a different sort of game. Normally Calumet was better than us and always savored victories against us and was known to run up the score. In fact, the year before our 1967 team, Calumet beat us by forty points. This year our record was twelve and two coming into the Calumet game. We had already beaten Crown Point, ranked number nine in the state.

Calumet had a poor team that year, so they were in for a shellacking. Of course their coach knew this and decided to do something quite different. After we got the opening tip and scored the first basket, Calumet went into a stall. They basically stalled the rest of the first quarter. They continued their stall in the second quarter, and the score at halftime was Griffith eight and Calumet two. A ton of the fans left at halftime as they were bored with the slow game. Coach told us at half that we were so much better than Calumet that we would show them by beating them at their own game. And Coach was so mad he had us come out in a stall in the third quarter. At that point most of the rest of the fans left. And we did show them. The game finally opened up a bit, but not much, with the final score being twenty-nine to twenty-two in favor of Griffith.

This game had special importance for me. One of Calumet's big guns was a kid named Freddie. Freddie had gone to elementary school with me and had always been a showoff—hotdog kind of a guy. Nothing had changed, so for Calumet in 1967 Freddie was a big gun on a bad team. He was guarding me as I got the ball near the top of the key on one of our possessions. I went to change directions on my dribble with my back to Griffith's basket and to Freddie. Freddie tried going around me to steal the ball. I gave him my best Earl the Pearl move as I changed hands and directions again and left him standing at the top of the key as I drove to the basket for an easy lay-in. So Freddie's night turned out not much better than Calumet's—not good.

———

The Gary Wirt game was unusual to say the least. I was a good shooter but tended to be streaky. When I got hot, I would make almost every shot. Well one of my buddies, Bill, had told me, "Ricky, you are just as good a shot and player as Kerry, Lenny, and Marty, so all you need to do is shoot the ball and you'll score a ton of points." I told Bill that wasn't our offense, but I also told Bill that if I ever got streaky hot in my shooting, I would shoot.

In the warm-ups before that Gary Wirt game, I didn't miss a shot. I not only was hot—I was on fire. So when we got the ball and came down the court for the first time, the ball was passed to me and I commenced to bury a twenty-foot jump shot. The defender was on me—went up with me but wasn't fast enough. The feeling of burying a twenty-foot jumper with someone all over you is like no other.

The next two times down the court the same thing occurred, and I knocked down two more twenty-foot jumpers to make it three in a row. All of these would have been three-point baskets today, but in 1967 they did not have three-point field goals. At that point Coach called time-out and said, "Butler, you're out of the game."

I said, "Why, Coach?"

Coach replied, "You seem to have forgotten our offense."

I said, "I'm hot, Coach!"

And Coach said, "You're not now—you're on the bench."

At halftime Coach was getting on the team because we were only leading by a couple of baskets and were shooting poorly. Coach said to the team, "You need to go out there and hit three in a row like Butler."

And I said in a low voice, "But if you do he'll take you out of the game".

But the voice wasn't low enough. Coach heard it and didn't like it. This managed to put me on Coach's shit list going into the state tournament. Not a good place to be.

Some of the guys on our team kind of sucked up to the coach to help their position on the team. I never did that with any of my coaches. This was probably because I'd heard Dad talk about him not sucking up to any of his bosses at work—which I might add did not do Dad's career any good. I remember at one point Dad not taking a job as a foreman because then he would have to spend all of his time sucking up to the big bosses. And later my dad was laid off—but he wouldn't have been if he'd have been a foreman. So at best I had an okay relationship with our coach, but at this point in the season my relationship with our coach was definitely headed south.

———

PANTHERS PLOT — Assistant coach Bud Wainscott discusses strategy with Tom Jamison (21), Rick Butler (15), Kerry Pickett (25) and Mike Schultrow as Griffith prepares for tonight with Clark.

STRATEGY TALK—Harold (Red) Mack, Griffith coach, talks his game plan with, left, Len Czapla, Pete Karnisky and Len Zarndt.

The Hammond Clark game was a tough one for me. Clark had one big gun on their team. He was six feet tall, fast, a good leaper, and he was their scoring machine. Coach decided to put me on him as I was

only an inch shorter, was a big jumper, and was one
of our better defensive players.

The first time down the court he got the ball
and went up for a jumper with me all over him. But
he made it—as he had a fast shot and I just missed
blocking it. This same thing happened the next two
times down the court as he hit three in a row on me.
The last one just grazed my fingertips but still went
in. Coach called time out, chewed me out, and took
me out of the game.

Well, I wasn't the only kid on our team who
couldn't guard this guy as he went on to score twenty-
two more points for a total of twenty-eight. But we
beat them anyway eighty-three to sixty-two. Coach
put me back in with the subs at the end of the game.
I played point guard, which was not my position,
but the game was put away and I scored a quick nine
points.

Lenny and Marty had good games, with each of
them scoring seventeen points. Skinner was stealing
the ball and was flying down the court on fast breaks,
and Marty was playing big in the middle on offense
and defense. I didn't have many rebounds that game,

but Marty had fifteen-plus—a good game for the
Foot.

DESPITE ABERCROMBIE

Griffith Coasts, 83-62

HAMMOND—When it comes to picking the surprise team of the year the Griffith Panthers will be right up there with the leaders.

Griffith concluded its regular season with an 83-62 drubbing of Hammond Clark here Tuesday night to run its record to an impressive 17-3. The Panthers have lost but once since Dec. 10, when they were downed by Gary Edison.

Coach Red Mack's crew then went on to rattle off nine consecutive victories, including the Crown Point holiday tourney championship. Two weeks ago Crown Point ended that streak and finished Griffith's Calumet Conference title hopes.

THE PANTHERS have bounced back to win their last five games and equal the previous best season mark at the school. Mack's 1963 unit also carried a 17-3 record into the sectional. That year, however, the Panthers were pitted in the East Chicago tourney. They lost in the first round to Hammond High.

As for this season, Mack had said that he would be happy to finish over .500. Well, the Panthers did, and in a manner that surprised even their most avid rooters.

"This team surprised everyone in the town," Mack said after Tuesday's game.

"NO MATTER what happens from here, this has been a tremendous year."

This doesn't mean that Mack's crew has reached a peak of self satisfaction, though.

This year Griffith is in the Crown Point sectional. The Hub affair looks to be an extremely well balanced tourney. The host school, Merrillville, and possibly Lowell, along with the Panthers have all shown definite signs of championship potential.

Griffith has split its two games with Crown Point and has drubbed Lowell, 95-66. Last week the Panthers subdued Merrillville with surprising ease, 73-55.

It was suggested to Mack that if the Panthers aren't ready for the tourney now, they never would be.

"WE'RE READY," answered Mack emphatically.

Against Clark, the Panthers were ready for anything. They used well-balanced scoring, four men in double figures, to overcome another gutty performance by Clark's Don Abercrombie. Abercrombie hit 28 points to run his season's average to an even 20 points per game, due mainly to a fantastic late season splurge.

Kerry Pickett and Marty Lehmann were high for Griffith with 17 points apiece. Len Zarndt hit 15 and Len Czapla chipped in 11.

The Pioneers concluded their schedule with a disappointing 4-16 mark.

Griffith (83)	FG	F	Pts.	Clark (62)	FG	F	Pts.
Butler	3	3-4	9	Aber'ble	12	4-5	28
Pickett	6	5-5	17	Rudz'nski	4	1-3	9
Lehmann	6	5-7	17	Ruf	1	0-0	2
Zarndt	4	7-7	15	Shimala	0	0-1	0
Czapla	5	1-1	11	King	3	1-1	7
Karnisky	1	0-0	2	Talaby	1	0-0	2
Schurkow	3	2-2	8	Win'ski	0	0-0	0
Jamiaba	0	0-3	0	Navta	0	5-8	0
Garrno	0	0-0	0	Mecklin	0	0-0	0
Britton	0	0-0	0	Solkey	0	4-6	4
Walters	0	4-5	4	Peters	0	0-1	0
				Hruskoci	0	0-0	0
Totals	28	27-31	83	Totals	26	18-37	62

SCORE BY QUARTERS

As we went through our long eleven-game winning streak, the excitement for the team was building, and we were also honoring our seniors during the home games. We had a large hoop with a paper Griffith panther drawn on it for our players to break through as we ran out onto the court. Each of us seniors was honored in turn to lead the team through the paper panther during those last home games. The place was packed as the whole town believed this was the year and we were the team they had been waiting for—a team of destiny. Excitement neared frenzied levels as we took turns leading our team through the paper panther.

I remember my turn. It was one of our last home games. As I prepared to lead the team out, my heart was pounding like it was before the first game that year. When I went out through the panther, the crowd went nuts—absolutely bonkers. What a rush to run out onto our home court and begin our warm-ups to the roar of the crowd. The feeling caused us to tingle with excitement and gave us goose bumps. As the crowd quieted, everything was magnified during those warm-ups, with the electrified crowd watching our every move. The sound of the basketball bouncing seemed to be enhanced. The squeak of those Converse All-Stars seemed crisper. And the swish of the net during our shooting practice was music to the ears. All eyes were on us as the excitement, expectations, the awesomeness of our accomplishments, the task ahead, all of that, became bigger than life. Hoosier hysteria at its best, and we were dead in the middle of it.

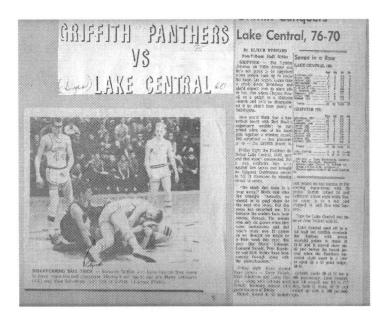

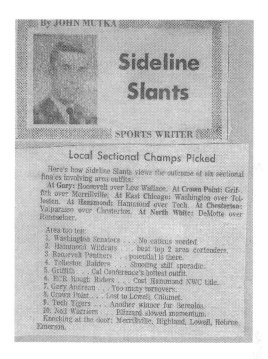

By JOHN MUTKA

Sideline Slants

SPORTS WRITER

Local Sectional Champs Picked

Here's how Sideline Slants views the outcome of six sectional finales involving area outfits:

At Gary: Roosevelt over Lew Wallace. At Crown Point: Griffith over Merrillville. At East Chicago: Washington over Tolleston. At Hammond: Hammond over Tech. At Chesterton: Valparaiso over Chesterton. At North White: DeMotte over Rensselaer.

Area top ten:

1. Washington Senators . . . No caucus needed.
2. Hammond Wildcats . . . beat top 2 area contenders.
3. Roosevelt Panthers . . . potential is there.
4. Tolleston Raiders . . . Shooting still sporadic.
5. Griffith . . . Cal Conference's hottest outfit.
6. ECR Rough Riders . . . Cost Hammond NWC title.
7. Gary Andrean . . . Too many turnovers.
8. Crown Point . . . Lost to Lowell, Calumet.
9. Tech Tigers . . . Another winner for Bereolos.
10. Noll Warriors . . . Blizzard slowed momentum.

Knocking at the door: Merrillville, Highland, Lowell, Hebron, Emerson.

Good Luck Panthers! Beat Hanover High!

Picture from school paper rooting on the
Panthers to do well in the state tourney

Sectional starting 5: Pete, Marty, Rick, Kerry, and Lenny dressing up as cheerleaders during a special pep rally prior to the state tournament sectional. Picture from school paper—*The Panther Press*

After finishing the regular season with seventeen wins and three losses, it was time for the state tournament. In Indiana in 1967, there were no classes based on school size. So for the state tournament, which started with the sectionals, it was luck of the draw as to which schools were paired to compete. This often resulted in big schools crushing the smaller schools. That's why we had never won our sectional and advanced to the regionals. We would always get beat by the bigger Gary and Hammond schools. But this year they had reconfigured the sectional pairings and we drew Hanover Central, a small rural school not far from us. This should have been an easy win for us, but the state tournament jitters set in and we struggled with this scrappy team. I started the game but didn't play well, with a bad case of the tournament jitters. My replacement, Mike, played better. We managed to win, but this was surely one of our worse games of the year. And there was some concern that this might shake our confidence going up against Crown Point in the sectional semifinal.

In fact Crown Point had recently beat us, breaking our eleven-game winning streak. But coach reassured the team that they'd just barely beat us and we had beaten them handily earlier in the year. Coach was confident we would avenge our loss.

My tournament jitters earned my replacement, Mike, the start against Crown Point. Mike played well against Crown Point and I played okay as a reserve but not quite good enough to earn back my starting role.

This turned out to be unfortunate for me, but more on that later.

Our team came out like gang-busters against Crown Point, having shaken the tourney jitters from the first game. We played a near-perfect first half with only one turnover. We dominated on offense, on defense, and in rebounding and had a commanding twenty-seven-point lead at half. We went on and cruised to a sixteen-point win, advancing to the sectional final game against Merrilville.

The victory over Crown Point left us beating that ninth-ranked team two out of three times that year. Although we never were ranked in the top ten, we clearly were right there, knocking on the door. Our coach never had a team as good as we were, and I'm not sure he quite knew what to do with us—but more on that later.

After Crown Point the sectional final game against Merrillville was almost a foregone conclusion. We coasted to a fifteen-point victory to seal the first-ever sectional championship in the history of our high school. I didn't start, played a fair amount, and did okay but again not that great.

———

Griffith Among 10 Newcomers To Regional Finals

East Chicago Regional Tournament Saturday, March 4

Gary Tolleston
12:30
Hammond Tech

Winner Game 1

Gary Roosevelt
1:45
Griffith

Winner Game 2

8:00   Championship

Marty and Rick (far side) carry their coach off the court in a jubilant sectional victory.

Marty and Rick (far side) carry their coach
off the court in a jubilant sectional victory.

The parade of cars back to our gym for a pep rally following the sectional was legendary. A string of cars almost two miles long paraded from Crown Point to Griffith. The gym was packed, and Coach had our team seated down at midcourt. He introduced every member of the varsity team and called our parents down to the court. He then mentioned a few things about each player. Coach commented on my speed as I raced down the court filling the lanes on fast breaks. He also said the players called me rabbit because I could jump so high.

Coach talked about Pete's great shot and how Marty and I were a couple of the best rebounders Griffith ever had. Coach said Marty was his "paint man" on offense and defense, a tremendous rebounder, and shot blocker extraordinaire. He also said that Lenny was an outstanding point guard, a team leader, and a player who had no quit. And of course he talked about our scoring machine—Kerry.

GRIFFITH TAKES SECTIONAL BASKETBALL TITLE

GRIFFITH – Left to right, front row: Don Schuster, manager, Rick Butler, Lennie Czapla, Leonard Zarndt, Pete Karnisky, Rick Garrard, and Gordon Dilling, manager. Back row: Coach Harold Mack, Asst. Coach, Bud Wain- scott, Mike Schultrow, Marty Lehman, Kerry Pickett, Tom Jamison, Tom Britton, Dave Walters, Floyd Davis, Athletic Director, and Ben McKay, Principal. Story on Sports Page.

Team picture at sectional victory rally

Griffith Captures Its First Sectional Crown

By JOHN MUTKA

Post-Tribune Sports Writer

CROWN POINT — It will be Panthers versus Panthers Saturday at the East Chicago regional.

Griffith's Panthers earned a shot at Gary Roosevelt's Panthers Saturday night by rebuffing Merrillville, 64-47, for their first sectional title in history.

Griffith shot .548 over the last three quarters (23 of 42) to notch its eighth straight victory in decisive fashion.

The Panthers, now 20-3, have lost only to Crown Point in their last 18 starts. That blemish was erased Saturday afternoon, 80-64.

Griffith abandoned its customary 1-2-2 zone after a Merrillville slowdown netted the Pirates a 6-2 advantage.

The Panthers switched to a on it the rest of the way with

Merrillville controlled the ball after the opening up for minutes before forward Wayne Svetanoff hit the first shot taken by his team.

Svetanoff scored six of the Pirates' first eight points and they struggled to an 11-9 lead at the end of the quarter.

Two free throws by lefty Marty Lehmann gave Griffith a 13-11 margin with 6:42 left in the half. Griffith took only three shots from the line in a half that sped by in a brisk 23 minutes. Neither team into the 1-and-1 situation and there were no substitutions until the second half started.

Griffith padded a 27-22 halftime lead to 35-24 with 5:32 remaining in the third period on three consecutive swishers by guard Pete Karnisky.

And that signalled the impending demise of the Pirates. The closest they could come was nine points down before bowing out with a 17-6 record.

Long Time Coming

GRIFFITH (64)

	Fgd	Fa	Ft	Pf
Pickett (25)	17	7	3-3	1
Schuttrow (13)	6	3	0-0	1
Lehmann (26)	6	3	4-5	1
Karnisky (14)	11	6	1-1	3
Zarndt (11)	3	7	1-3	2
Czecla (10)	0	0	0-0	0
Butler (15)	5	1	1-5	0
Jamison (21)	0	0	0-0	0
Totals	55	27	10-17	9

MERRILLVILLE (47)

	Fgd	Fg	Ft	Pf
Svetanoff (44)	9	7	2-2	2
Crnovich (20)	8	5	0-0	1
Sorrick (34)	16	5	1-1	1
Aten (22)	6	2	3-5	4
Hill (10)	7	2	1-2	0
Lester (24)	5	0	0-0	0
Simic (42)	4	2	0-0	0
Gahovan (14)	0	0	0-0	0
Idbar (13)	0	0	0-0	0
Abel (30)	0	0	0-0	0
Totals	57	20	7-13	11

Griffith	9	18	17	20—64
Merrillville	11	11	10	15—47

Officials — Walter Swift, Albica; John Ward, Brookston.

Errors — Merrillville 13, Griffith 10.

A layup by Rick Crnovich trimmed Griffith's lead to 37-328, but the Panthers took a 44-32 lead by swishing seven of 17 shots in the third period.

Griffith put together a 12-2 spurt to open a 62-41 advantage with less than four minutes to play.

The superbly-balanced Panthers were paced by a 17-point blast by Kerry Pickett. Clever playmaker Len Zarndt, the club's stylish floor general, added 15 and two other teammates finished in double figures.

This is how the scoreboard looked following the end of the 1967 sectional tournament. Griffith Panthers defeated Merrillville by a large margin of 17 points

A GREAT SECTIONAL — Rick Butler, of the Panthers takes his turn at cutting a souvenir of the sectional net at Crown Point when Griffith defeated Merrillville to win the sectional crown. (Journal Photo)

Winning the sectional was a crowning achievement for all of the players. However, more work lay ahead of us in the regionals.

Unfortunately we drew Gary Roosevelt in the first pairings of the regional. Gary Roosevelt had an enrollment of two thousand students compared to our six hundred and had consistently been ranked in the top five state schools all year. Gary Roosevelt's front line averaged six foot five compared to our six foot two. I was five foot eleven.

The score was similarly unbalanced, with Roosevelt winning by over twenty points.

———

This concluded a Cinderella season for the 1967 Griffith hoopsters with a final record of twenty and four and our first-ever sectional championship in the Indiana State High School tournament. We made basketball history at Griffith that year to be sure.

Our high school gave the whole school a day off to celebrate. I'll never forget in my history class our teacher had the basketball players in his class stand up. He commenced to say how we had made basketball history for Griffith by winning the first-ever sectional championship. As me and another player stood, he looked at us and told the whole class that it was one thing to study history but another to make history and all the basketball players had just earned an A in his class.

He wasn't kidding—we all got As. And do you think any of the other kids complained? Not one word. It was almost like we were gods—the way we were treated with everyone slapping us on the backs, congratulating us, and even hugs from many of the girls. We ate it up as we basked in the glory we had earned through thousands of hours on the basketball courts. This was a dream of a lifetime—a dream come true.

As for me, my tournament jitters in the first game of the sectional and being somewhat on the coach's shit list probably cost me a college scholarship. Following my poor start in game one, I didn't start in the last three games of the tournament. I got playing time but not enough to impress the college scouts, who were out in droves for the state tournament. Marty ended up with a scholarship to Valdosta State College in Valdosta, Ga. Lenny got a scholarship at UNLV in Las Vegas. But no scouts talked to me. Had I played in the state tournament anywhere close to how I played in the holiday tournament, I might well have had a scholarship, which would have changed my life.

Our coach had made a comment in the paper that although our team was great, he still felt that next year's team would be even better. He was dead wrong as next year Griffith did not have as winning a regular season, nor did they win the sectional. This further reaffirmed the theory that he did not know how good we were. And there are those who would say there was no way we could ever beat Roosevelt by running with them. Their game was run and gun, and we played into their hands by running our fast-break offense. And there were some who said we had a legitimate chance of beating them had we slowed the game down. Irrespective, we did lose, but we still had the best season in the history of our school, and our coach played a huge role in our success.

Our 1967 Griffith Panther basketball team led our whole town of Griffith on a beautiful ride through Hoosier hysteria at its best. As for me and my team-mates, we were dead in the middle of all of that, and we loved and cherished every minute of it. We had put in so much time and effort on the basketball courts to make this happen. But make no mistake, it was a labor of love. Few people ever live their dreams, but we sure did—a dream come true for every one of us. And we were honored to have been able to do this—for the love of the game …

The End

Postscript—Post High School Basketball

My post high school basketball was quite limited. My family was of modest means, so although most of my friends were going away to college, I was enrolled in the local extension of Indiana University and was staying home. My girlfriend, Judy, was also going away to college in Minnesota. So with no college scouts talking to me, I realized that my basketball career was pretty much over. And as I was starting to feel left behind, I woke up one morning and decided to join the army, which would get me "going away" too.

Well little did I know that this army would not turn out to be the army with all of the adventures that were portrayed so gloriously by John Wayne and the movies. Rather, this army turned out to be the one that would take me to the jungles of Vietnam and all the horrors of war at the ripe old age of eighteen. Ironically, I did play a little pick-up ball in a few of the base camps that had been carved out of the jungles. One of my paratrooper buddies, Paul, had played high school basketball in Kansas and was a pretty good player. He and I would play a little round ball when we were back in base camp. But mostly we were infantry paratroopers, out in the jungle, involved in combat operations. I often wondered what happened to Paul after Vietnam. I figured he probably went to college as he was a sharp guy. But I knew he did not end up playing college basketball—not with having his foot blown off near the end of his scheduled return from Vietnam.

Ironically, the army almost gave me a big chance to play post-high school ball for the Fort Knox army team. My first sergeant at Fort Knox turned out to be the coach of Fort Knox's basketball team. One day the first sergeant overheard me talking to one of the guys about playing high school basketball in Indiana. He called me into his office and closed the door. He said he had overheard me talking about playing basketball in Indiana. He asked me to tell him about our team.

I told him about our best-ever season, finishing with a record of twenty wins and four losses, and being beat in the state tournament by Gary Roosevelt, who went to the state championship final game. I told him I played small forward but was fast and could jump—averaging ten to fifteen rebounds a game and ten points. I said I could have scored more but our offense centered on Kerry, and my role was to feed the scoring machine. I also said I was one of the better defensive guys on the team.

The first sergeant listened to all of this, asked a few more questions, and told me he wanted me on his team and that I would be a big part of that team. He wanted me to come to the gym for a small tryout that next week for me to show him my stuff. He told me that his players played a lot more basketball than army. I said I loved basketball, and the first sergeant said he could tell.

But some things are not meant to be. That weekend I came down with two different types of malaria at the same time. I was in the hospital for two weeks, followed by a forty-five-day convalescent leave to get my strength back. In the meantime the team was set, but there was no way I could have played anyway. I had not fully recovered and was still weakened from malaria.

I went to college at the University of Minnesota, Duluth, which had an enrollment of five thousand students. I surely could have played basketball there. But I had no time as I had to work full-time even in spite of the GI bill. In fact, given I had to pay out-of-state tuition my first year, I worked anywhere from thirty-two to forty-eight hours a week while going to school full-time.

After graduating from college with an accounting degree, I became a CPA and worked for Ernst & Young (Ernst & Ernst then) in Minneapolis. My interest in accounting started with my bookkeeping class my senior year in high school. Immediately I took a liking to the subject and actually looked forward to my homework, which involved posting accounting transactions to journals, ledgers, etc. My best friend, Marty, was in my class, and Marty hated bookkeeping. One day when Marty was over at my house, I was posting my transactions with such enthusiasm that Marty said, "Rab, looks like you really enjoy posting your journals." I confirmed that I did. Marty commenced to ask me if I wanted to help him post his transactions. And I said, "Sure, I'll do that." Don't know how much this ended up helping Marty, but I got a ninety-nine on the final exam in that class. My teacher encouraged me to go into accounting as he had never had a student do nearly that well on his final exam.

Shortly after joining Ernst and Young, I found out that the firm rented a local high school gym every Monday night for pick-up basketball games. This became my first opportunity to play any significant amount of basketball since high school, seven years before. Many of the guys who played in these pick-up games had played college basketball in division II and III colleges. Someone asked me if I had played in college. I said no, and it was suggested I might not want to play against these guys as they were good and I might be in over my head. My immediate answer was that I thought I could still play and would be fine. This probably seemed like overconfidence or cockiness on my part. Surely after seven years I would not be able to compete with guys who had played college ball as recently as a couple of years before. But I was a Hoosier basketball player, and the hysteria was still alive and well inside of me.

I arrived at the first Monday night game a little early so I could practice my shooting and a little ball handling. I was rusty, but after about ten or fifteen minutes it pretty much came back and I started knocking down twenty-foot jumpers as I started feeling something I had not felt for seven years. I felt the resurgence of my love for the game.

I did well in that first pick-up Monday night game, although I became winded as I was nowhere close to game shape. Irrespective, I could play with all of these guys. Afterward, one of the better guys asked me where I had played college ball. My response was Vietnam U. I went on to explain how I had played high school basketball in Indiana on basically a state-ranked team. I had gone on to be a paratrooper in Vietnam and didn't play in college as I had to work.

As I played more and more Monday night pick-up games and started jogging as well, my conditioning came back. And when it did, I was one of the better players on the court. I heard some of the college ball players saying that it was hard to believe I hadn't played college ball and had basically not played for seven years. These guys had been starters at smaller Minnesota colleges, such as St John's, Mankato State, and St. Cloud State. What these guys didn't know is that I had played a lifetime's worth of basketball in the first eighteen years of my life. The quality of play for me and my senior year's team was the equivalent of many division II college basketball teams and most division III teams. When you play a lifetime's worth of basketball in Indiana by age eighteen, you don't forget how to play—not in seven years, not even in a lifetime.

I left Ernst & Young, moved to Apple Valley, Minnesota, and went to work for Pepsi. I put a basketball backboard, rim, and net on my garage and would shoot around occasionally. One time as I was knocking down twenty-foot jumpers, my neighbor, Craig, came over and asked me if I had played basketball in school. (Craig had been a professional baseball player for the Minnesota Twins.) I told him about my Indiana basketball, and Craig invited me to join his "over thirty" league. I played on Craig's team that year and again was one of the better players in the league.

I played on a couple of other teams over the next two years and finally formed my own team with some of the best players from the other teams I had been on. We were very good but unfortunately the play was rough, and in the fourth game I was pushed when I was way up for a rebound. When I came down, my leg bent sideways at the knee—and that was the end of my season. As it turned out, that was the end of my league play as well. The second-best player on our team had his knee blown out the next game, so the team kind of fell apart and did not do well.

A car accident hurt that same knee. This time it was bad, with one cartilage shattered, another torn, and I had ruptured my ACL. So my league play was clearly done. And mostly my basketball was done—until I coached my son, Doug, and my granddaughter, Maya.

My son, Doug, loved to shoot hoops with me in the driveway. Ultimately Doug played basketball in the community league. I was traveling and was busy with my work so I initially did not have the time to help coach Doug's team. In Doug's fifth-grade season, Doug's coach needed an assistant, so I agreed to help. Well, as it turned out the head coach had to travel a lot too and ended up missing more games than he coached. So I became quite involved with the team, and Doug had a very good year. He scored his share of points and was clearly the best rebounder on his team and often on the court in spite of the fact that he wasn't all that tall. At the end of the season the head coach handed out awards to each player. Doug got the "Mr. Rebounder" award. Once again I could feel the surge of my love for the game. This time it was through my son.

Unfortunately, the next year was Doug's last as a basketball player. Doug's asthma had gotten worse. During the first few games of Doug's sixth-grade year, he had bad asthma attacks during the games. He had to be taken to the emergency room the last time. This one was scary as Doug was blue by the time they got him breathing well again. I knew this was it. No more basketball for Doug. So his promising career was cut short by the sixth grade.

Doug taking a jump shot

Doug

———

When my granddaughter, Maya, was six, she was watching me shoot baskets in my driveway. She asked if she could shoot too. I got a basketball goal that would allow the rim to be adjusted to different heights. Maya first started shooting at a six-foot rim. She said she wanted to play in the community basketball league starting in the fall. So later in the summer, I raised our basket to eight feet, the height of the rims in the community basketball league. I signed her up for a team, and Maya played her first organized basketball at the young age of six. I did not coach the team but watched Maya as she developed her skills and love for the game.

The next year I was an assistant coach on her team. Their team did okay, and Maya did fine.

The following year when Maya was eight, I became the head coach of her team. Unfortunately the teams had not been properly balanced, as four of the eight girls on her team had not previously played any basketball. This proved to be a challenge to say the least, as our team managed to eke out only three wins out of ten season games. In spite of the team's poor performance, Maya had fun and was not discouraged.

The next year I was a co-coach with the mother of one of the other girls on Maya's team. By this time Maya was becoming quite skilled. She could dribble the ball with both hands, and I had taught her to be a rebounder. Maya was one of the better players in the league, and it really showed up in the tournament at the end of the year as their team made a run—winning a couple of games and advancing to the quarter finals.

In their last game, Maya played as if she was possessed. She was all over the court, dribbling the ball down, rebounding, and scoring. She was knocked down a few times, the last time with seventeen seconds to go in the game. She was down at midcourt, and she was crying.

I went out on the court to get her, and she said it was her knee. I asked her if it was that bad that she was crying. (She had been knocked down many times before but never cried.) Maya said her knee wasn't that bad but they were losing by six points with only seventeen seconds to go. They were going to lose, which would end their season. I could once again feel the surge from the love for the game—this time through Maya.

I had planted the seeds well as the next year Maya tried out and made the fifth-grade traveling team. I did not coach this team as the game had changed and I felt the younger coaches could do a better job. Besides, now my love for the game could continue vicariously through Maya. Maya was not born a Hoosier, but somehow my Hoosier hysteria had rubbed off on her. The love for the game was in her blood.

Maya—bottom right

Maya—top right

What Became of the Senior '67 Hoopster Panthers and Their Coach

Coach retired from teaching and coaching three years after our '67 team. Marty had a discussion with Coach about the '67 season after Coach retired. Coach told Marty this was his best team ever, and there were many reasons for the success of this team:

- The players loved basketball and even practice. Every practice was 100 percent effort, and the team never had a bad practice.
- Every player put the team before individual desires and achievements.
- All the players got along well and accepted their roles for the good of the team.
- The team had great rebounding, with Marty, Rick, and Kerry dominating both the defensive and offensive boards
- Team speed was a key to success. The team was fast, and we fast breaked throughout the entire game. This resulted in easy baskets, especially toward the end of the game as the defense

tired. It also produced a tremendous offense, averaging seventy-plus points per game.

- The town of Griffith so loved this team that people came to watch practice. This was basically unheard of and had never happened with any of Coach's teams.

- Our point guard, Lenny, was a great leader. He worked extremely hard and expected the same from all of the players, and Skinner got it.

- The team played great defense. Many players who are "stat conscious" (concerned about scoring, etc.) don't play much defense as it is tiring and does not show up in the stats. But not us; we played tough defense, which set up our fast-breaking offense.

- We finally won our sectional, and we deserved it as we were a great team.

- Although we were knocked out of the state tournament in the regionals, we were beat by Gary Roosevelt, who had been consistently rated as one of the top teams in the state throughout the year. We were never rated in the top ten in the state because two of our three regular-season losses came in the first five games of the season. By the end of the year, we had beaten Crown Point two out of three games, and they had been rated number nine in the state. So clearly, we were one of the top teams in the whole state of Indiana (big and small schools alike). We were a small school (enrollment of around six hundred) with a basketball team that had a big heart. And our town of Griffith totally loved us. Hoosier hysteria at its best …

Lenny (Skinner—our point guard)

Lenny went to college at the University of Nevada—Las Vegas (UNLV) with a full basketball scholarship. Lenny graduated with a degree in elementary education and went on to teach first graders for thirty-plus years. Lenny now is retired with his wife, Donna, and resides in Las Vegas.

Marty (Foot—our center)

Marty went to college at Valdosta St. College in Valdosta, Georgia, with a full basketball scholarship. Marty, like Lenny, majored in elementary education and taught school in Georgia for a few years after graduation. Marty then returned to Griffith, Indiana, where he went back to school, earning an associate's degree in industrial engineering. Marty worked construction, mostly as a field engineer traveling throughout the country on various jobs. Marty is now retired and lives near Orlando, Florida, with his wife, Kay.

Pete (Nisky—our shooting guard)

Pete was the best and purest shooter on that team. He could knock down open twenty-foot jumpers like there was no tomorrow—nothing but net. Pete was a member of the student council, a class officer, and homecoming king our senior year. Pete was a great guy who everyone liked. Pete went to college at Purdue University. He tried out for the basketball team his freshman year and made it to the last cut but did not make the team. And making it to the final cut in a Big 10 school is no small feat and was a testament to Pete's basketball ability. Pete graduated with an accounting/business degree, and he worked as a CPA for Price Waterhouse (one of the big national CPA firms) for a number of years. He then worked for Oscar Meyer in Madison, Wisconsin, before relocating to the

Orlando, Florida, area. In Florida, Pete worked as a hospital administrator and ultimately as a real estate developer and home builder. Pete passed away on July 11, 2008, and is dearly missed by his classmates and basketball buddies. Pete, thanks for the memories …

Tom Jamison (power forward and a reserve player)

Tom is married and still resides in the Griffith area. Tom had a rewarding career with Indiana Bell, from which Tom is now retired.

Rick (Rabbit—our small forward)

Rick spent three years in the army and was a paratrooper in Vietnam in 1968. Following the army Rick went to the University of Minnesota, Duluth, where, like Pete, Rick earned an accounting/business degree. Rick also went to work at one of the big national CPA firms (Ernst & Young). Rick then went on to work for Pepsi and ultimately for the *Star Tribune* newspaper in Minneapolis as a senior finance manager/director. Rick is now retired and living with his high school sweetheart and wife of forty-plus years, Judy. Rick and Judy reside in Rosemount,

Minnesota. Rick has also turned into a writer of sorts. Rick wrote his Vietnam memoirs after forty years—*POINT—A Paratrooper's Memoirs of Vietnam*, which was published in December of 2007 and of course, this book.

The 1967 Griffith Panther Basketball Team

Printed in the United States
By Bookmasters